THE ROYAL COURT THEATRE PRESENTS

G

By Tife Kusoro

G was first performed at the Royal Court Jerwood Theatre Upstairs, Sloane Square, on Thursday 22 August 2024.

G
By Tife Kusoro

Cast (in alphabetical order)

Kai **Selorm Adonu**
Joy **Kadiesha Belgrave**
Khaleem **Ebenezer Gyau**
Baitface **Dani Harris-Walters**

Director **Monique Touko**
Designer **Madeleine Boyd**
Lighting Designer **Adam King**
Sound Designer **Khalil Madovi**
Video Designer **Tyler Forward**
Movement Director & Choreographer **Kloé Dean**
Costume Designer & Supervisor **Rianna Azoro**
Casting Director **Jatinder Chera**
Production Manager **Ian Taylor**
Stage Manager **Nick Graham**
Deputy Stage Manager **Stacey Nurse**

From the Royal Court, on this production:

Stage Supervisor **Steve Evans**
Lighting Supervisor **Lucinda Plummer**
Lighting & Video Technician **Daisy Simmons**
Video Supervisors **Daisy Simmons & Deanna Towli**
Lighting Programmer **Lizzie Skellett**
Company Manager **Mica Taylor**
Lead Producer **Ralph Thompson**

G is a co-production with SISTER.

Tife Kusoro (Writer)

For the Royal Court: SW1 Project, My White Best Friend (and Other Letters Left Unsaid), Living Newspaper Edition 2.

Other theatre includes: We Have Sinned (45North); Butterfly (Talawa).

Awards include: George Devine Award (G), Royal Court Lynne Gagliano Writers' Award.

Selorm Adonu (Kai)

Theatre includes: Brother's Keeper (Theatre Peckham); Anthem (Almeida).

Television includes: Curfew, Casualty.

As writer and performer, short film includes: Man to Man.

Rianna Azoro (Costume Designer & Supervisor)

For the Royal Court: seven methods of killing kylie jenner.

As Costume Designer, theatre includes: GIRLS (New Diorama).

As Costume Supervisor, other theatre includes: The Hot Wing King (National); An Unfinished Man (Yard); A Number (Old Vic); The Wife of Willesden, Snowflake, The Half God of Rainfall (& Birmingham Rep) (Kiln); Cymbeline, Julius Caesar (LAMDA); J'Ouvert, Nine Night (& National) (West End); The Tyler Sisters (Hampstead); Amsterdam (Orange Tree); Chiaroscuro, Strange Fruit (Bush); Richard II (Globe); The Emperor (& TFANA New York), And Yet It Moves (Young Vic).

As Wardrobe Manager or Dresser, theatre includes: The Woman in White, 9 to 5 (West End); Roller Diner (Soho); Filthy Business, The Haystack (Hampstead); Twelfth Night [& Assistant Costume Supervisor], Terma (& Park Avenue Armory), Wings, Life of Galileo (Young Vic).

As Costume Designer, film includes: Caesar Salad, Comedy Central PEP TALK, Curveball [Associate Costume Designer].

As Costume Supervisor, TV and film includes: So Beano, Together.

As Costume Assistant, TV and film includes: Peacock, Aipro AD, Vodafone Sledge AD, Gojek AD, Three Recharge, Fever, When The West Is Done With You, DOLAPO IS FINE, The Rooftop.

Kadiesha Belgrave (Joy)

Theatre includes: Grud (Hampstead).

Television includes: Haven, Sleepover.

Short films include: Lizard, Only Child.

Madeleine Boyd (Designer)

Theatre includes: Gone Too Far! (Stratford East); L'Histoire du Soldat (Maggio Musicale); My Fair Lady, A Little Night Music (Leeds Playhouse/Opera North); Lady in the Dark (Opera Zuid); Liebelei (Voralberger Theater).

Opera includes: A Quiet Place (Opera Zuid); Lalla Roukh (Wexford Festival Opera); Raising Icarus (Birmingham Rep); Donizetti Trilogy: Anna Bolena, Maria Stuarda, Roberto Devereux (& Teatro Real Madrid) (Welsh National Opera); La Traviata (& Opera Israel/Komische Oper Berlin/Cape Town Opera), Don Giovanni, Turn of the Screw (Opera North); Macbeth (Grange Festival); Carmen (Nikikai Foundation/Tour); Wuthering Heights, Semiramide (Opera National de Lorraine); The Merry Widow, Rigoletto, Andre Chenier, The Voyage of Edgar Allen Poe (Staatstheater Braunschweig); Mamzer Bastard (& Hackney Empire); Glare (ROH); Mitridate (Rokokotheater Schloss); Margherita d'Anjou (Festival della Valle d'Itria); Albert Herring (Opera di Firenze/ Maggio Musicale); Fidelio (Longborough Festival Opera); Powder Her Face (Royal Danish Opera Copenhagen); La Cenerentola (Teatro Regio/Malmo Opera); Oresteia (Sosnoff Theatre/Bard Summerscape); Turandot (Staatstheater Augsburg Open Air Arena).

As Art Director, film includes: We Have Always Lived In The Castle (trailer).

Awards include: 2 Place de L'Opera Awards for Best Opera (Lady in the Dark, A Quiet Place), Irish Times Theatre Awards for Best Costume (Lalla Roukh), Arets Reumert Prize for Best Opera Production (Powder Her Face).

Jatinder Chera (Casting Director)

Theatre includes: The Comeuppance (Almeida); The P Word, Sleepova, A Playlist for the Revolution, The Real Ones (Bush); The Flea, Samuel Takes a Break, Multiple Casualty Incident (Yard); Sweat (Royal Exchange).

Kloé Dean (Movement Director & Choreographer)

Theatre includes: Boy At The Back Of The Class (Rose Theatre/Tour); Breakin' Convention (Sadler's Wells); Doughnuts & Ice Cream (Catford Broadway); Everything I Own (Brixton House); Gone Too Far!, Tambo and Bones (Stratford East); Tapped (Theatre503); Scar Test (LAMDA); Hungry (Soho); Dorian (Reading Rep); Really Big and Really Loud, Black Love, May Queen (Paines Plough/ Roundabout).

Film includes: Nakhane – Tell Me Your Politik (feat. Moonchild Sanelly & Nile Rodgers), Arrive Like You Mean It (ASDA), I Want Choo (Jimmy Choo), Love Sweet Love (Little Mix), Introvert (Little Simz), Woman (Little Simz), Sweet Blue (Cleo Sol), One (Cleo Sol), The Heavy Grown (Plan UK).

Live performance includes: Brit Awards: Little Simz, Capital FM Summertime Ball: Anne Marie, MOBO Awards: Ghetts, Capital FM Summertime Ball: Nathan Dawe, Radio 1 Big Weekend: Anne Marie, Wizkid – Made in Lagos @ O2 Arena, Later... with Jools Holland: Little Simz Woman.

Tyler Forward (Video Designer)

As Designer, theatre includes: **Dorian The Musical** (Southwark Playhouse); **Sunday In Park with George** (Mack); **Redcliffe** (Turbine); **Diana The Musical Concert** (Eventim Apollo); **Trompe L'Oiel** (The Other Palace); **Loserville** (Blackheath Halls); **Our House** (The Albany); **No Man's Island, Redemption, Mission** (The Big House); **Play, The Games** (P&O Arvia); **Silence** (Donmar/Tara); **Musical Theatre Showcase** (Trinity Laban); **Roles We'll Never Play, Close Quarter** (West End); **Opening Up: The Mental Health Musical** (Union); **Thoroughly Modern Millie** (Electric); **Nor Woman Neither** (Tristan Bates); **Macbeth** (Vanbrugh); **Stoning Mary** (George Bernard Shaw).

As Associate Designer, theatre includes: **Burlesque The Musical** (UK Premiere); **Carlos Acosta's Nutcracker** (Tour); **Umm Kulthum & The Goldern Era** (Bahrain National); **Once The Musical Concert** (Tour); **Kenneth Branagh's King Lear** (West End); **The House With Chicken Legs** (Tour); **The Trials** (Marlowe), **Spongebob The Musical** (Tour); **Umm Kulthum & The Goldern Era** (Ithra).

As Designer, exhibitions include: **Wes Anderson's Asteroid City Exhibition, Future Shock.**

As Associate Designer, exhibitions include: **Wes Anderson's French Dispatch.**

Nick Graham (Stage Manager)

As Stage Manager, theatre includes: **The Yellow Wallpaper** (Coronet); **Woke, The Creature, Out of the Dark** (Rose); and numerous shows for Polka.

As Company Stage Manager, theatre includes: **Self Raising** (Queen Dome); **The Dry House** (Marylebone); **Sarah** (Coronet); **Beauty & The Beast** (Rose).

As Assistant Stage Manager, theatre includes: **Leopards** (Rose).

Tech Support includes: **Festival of Taiwanese Culture, Tiger is Coming, Electric Japan** (Coronet); **In Theatre** (Bricklane).

Ebenezer Gyau (Khaleem)

Theatre includes: **Dear England** (National).

Television includes: **Suspect.**

Film includes: **County Lines.**

Short film includes: **That Night, Held.**

Dani Harris-Walters (Baitface)

Dance includes: **Black Victorians** (Tour); **Blak Whyte Gray** (Barbican); **Born To Manifest** (Tour); **Born To Protest** (Tour); **Breakin' Convention** (Sadlers' Wells); **Fagin's Twist** (The Place); **Illegal Dance** (Tour); **The Black Album** (Tour).

As Writer and Performer, theatre includes: **Happy Father's Day** (The Place).

Film includes: **Little Simz - Introvert, Laura Mvula - Overcome, Edem Wornoo - Grey, MckNasty - Not Nice** (feat. Kojey Radical), **White X - Leah Mcfall, Smythson - Journey To The Wild Side.**

Live performances includes: **Brit Awards: Little Simz, The Graham Norton Show: Laura Mvula, X-Factor: Elle Goulding, London 2012 Olympic Games Opening Ceremony: 'Second to the right, and straight on till morning', Sault: Sault - Acts of Faith.**

Adam King (Lighting Designer)

Theatre includes: **Harry Potter & The Cursed Child** [Assistant Lighting Designer], **Bend it like Beckham** [Assistant Lighting Designer] (West End); **Fun at the Bach, Then, Now & Next, Sappho, Unfortunate The Untold Story Of Ursula The Sea Witch** (& Tour) (Southwark Playhouse); **Legends The Divas** (Tour); **Flowers for Mrs Harris** (Riverside Studios); **Annie Get Your Gun** (Lavender Theatre); **We Need New Names** (Tour); **Gone Too Far!** (Stratford East); **From Here to Eternity, The Milk Train Doesn't Stop Here Anymore** (Charing Cross); **Flashdance** (European Tour); **Snowflake/Tornado** (Tour/BBC); **Dare You Say Please** (King's Head); **We're Few And Far Between** (White Bear); **How to Survive an Apocalypse** (Finborough); **Robin Hood, Jack & the Beanstalk, Aladdin** (Harlow Playhouse); **The Nutcracker, Peter Pan, Beauty & the Beast** (New Theatre Royal Portsmouth); **The Clockmakers Daughter** (Cadogan Hall); **Beyond Therapy** (Tour); **Original Death Rabbit, The Wasp** (Jermyn Street); **Gentlemen Prefer Blondes, Lysistrata Jones** (Andrew Lloyd Webber Foundation); **Sunday in the Park with George, Caucasian Chalk Circle, 9 to 5, Urinetown, Oh What A Lovely War, The Little Mermaid, Enron, Legally Blonde, Coram Boy, Shakespeare in Love, Hamlet, Macbeth, Guys & Dolls** (Mack).

Ballet includes: **Fieldworks, Assemblage, Mephisto Waltz, Swingle Stepping, Fast Blue** (ROH).

TV includes: **Basic Lee, Snowflake/Tornado.**

Khalil Madovi (Sound Designer)

Theatre includes: **Red Pitch** (Bush/West End); **No More Mr. Nice Guy, Brenda's Got A Baby** (& New Diorama) (Nouveau Riche); **Can I Live?** (Complicité/Barbican); **Gone Too Far!** (Stratford East); **Soundclash: Death in the Arena** (Edinburgh Fringe); **This Is What The Journey Does** (Old Vic); **The Poison Belt** (Jermyn Street).

Stacey Nurse (Deputy Stage Manager)

As Assistant Stage Manager, for the Royal Court: **For Black Boys Who Have Considered Suicide When The Hue Gets Too Heavy (& West End/New Diorama/Nouveau Riche).**

As Stage Manager, other theatre includes: **Between The Lines (& The Big House), Brenda's Got a Baby (New Diorama); I Love You Now What?, Blueprints (Pleasance/ Edinburgh Fringe), Summer Camp for Broken People (Summerhall/Edinburgh Fringe); The Tinker (VAULTS) Inscribed in Me [& Re-lighter], Mapping Gender [Technical Stage Manager] (REcreate Agency).**

As Assistant Stage Manager, theatre includes: **Future Cargo [ASM Cover] (The Place).**

As Lighting Designer, theatre includes: **Surrender (Arcola).**

As Production Manager, Lighting and Video Designer, theatre includes: **When This Is Over (New Diorama/ Camden People's).**

As Assistant Production Manager, theatre includes: **Dance No 2 (The Place).**

As Production LX, dance includes: **Matthew Bourne's Sleeping Beauty (Sadler's Wells).**

Ian Taylor (Production Manager)

Theatre includes: **Fiddler on the Roof (Regent's Park Open Air); A Chorus of Disapproval (Salisbury Playhouse); Kim's Convenience, The Marilyn Conspiracy (Park); The Hypochondriac, Accidental Death of an Anarchist (Sheffield); The Way Old Friends Do, Tartuffe (Birmingham Rep); Here, The Funeral Director, Trestle, Orca, After Independence, Tom Cat (Papatango); A Single Man, Sweet Science of Bruising, Rasheda Speaking, Dear Brutus (Troupe).**

Opera Includes: **Albert Herring (Royal Academy of Music); Pandora's Box, Ever Young, Shadowtracks, The Cutlass Crew, Eliza & the Swans, Deep Waters, The Fizz (London Youth Opera/W11); The Power of Paternal Love, Raising Icarus, L'Agrippina (Barber Opera); Goulio Cesare, Cosi Fan Tutte (Bury Court Opera); Oedipus Rex and L'Enfant et Les Sortilèges (The Philharmonia Orchestra).**

Monique Touko (Director)

Theatre includes: **School Girls; Or, the African Mean Girls Play, Wedding Band: A Love/Hate Story in Black and White (Lyric Hammersmith); The Boy at the Back of the Class (Tour); We Need New Names (Tour); Gone Too Far! (Stratford East); The Clinic (Almeida); Fair Play (Bush); Malindadzimu (Hampstead).**

THE ROYAL COURT THEATRE

The Royal Court Theatre is the writers' theatre. It is a leading force in world theatre for cultivating and supporting writers - undiscovered, emerging and established.

Since 1956, we have commissioned and produced hundreds of writers, from John Osborne to Mohamed-Zain Dada. Royal Court plays from every decade are now performed on stages and taught in classrooms and universities across the globe.

Through the writers, the Royal Court is at the forefront of creating restless, alert, provocative theatre about now. We open our doors to the unheard voices and free thinkers that, through their writing, change our way of seeing.

We strive to create an environment in which differing voices and opinions can co-exist. In current times, it is becoming increasingly difficult for writers to write what they want or need to write without fear, and we will do everything we can to rise above a narrowing of viewpoints.

Through all our work, we strive to inspire audiences and influence future writers with radical thinking and provocative discussion.

🐦 royalcourt ⑤ royalcourttheatre

Supported using public funding by
ARTS COUNCIL ENGLAND

ROYAL COURT SUPPORTERS

Our incredible community of supporters makes it possible for us to achieve our mission of nurturing and platforming writers at every stage of their careers. Our supporters are part of our essential fabric – they help to give us the freedom to take bigger and bolder risks in our work, develop and empower new voices, and create world-class theatre that challenges and disrupts the theatre ecology.

To all our supporters, thank you. You help us to write the future.

PUBLIC FUNDING

ARTS COUNCIL ENGLAND

CHARITABLE PARTNERS

BackstageTrust

COCHAYNE

T. S. ELIOT FOUNDATION

JERWOOD FOUNDATION

TRUSTS & FOUNDATIONS

Maria Björnson Memorial Fund
Martin Bowley Charitable Trust
Chalk Cliff Trust
The Noël Coward Foundation
Cowley Charitable Foundation
The Davidson Play GC Bursary
The Lynne Gagliano Writers' Award
The Golden Bottle Trust
The Harold Hyam Wingate Foundation
John Lyon's Charity
The Marlow Trust
Clare McIntyre's Bursary
Old Possum's Practical Trust
Richard Radcliffe Charitable Trust
Rose Foundation
Royal Victoria Hall Foundation
The Thistle Trust
The Thompson Family Charitable Trust

CORPORATE SPONSORS & SUPPORTERS

Aqua Financial Ltd
Cadogan
Concord Theatricals
Edwardian Hotels, London
Prime Time
Sustainable Wine Solutions
Walpole

SISTER

CORPORATE MEMBERS

Bloomberg Philanthopies
Sloane Stanley

INDIVIDUAL SUPPORTERS

Artistic Director's Circle

Katie Bradford
Jeremy & Becky Broome
Clyde Cooper
Debbie De Girolamo &
  Ben Babcock
Denzil Fernandez
Dominique & Neal Gandhi
Lydia & Manfred Gorvy
David & Jean Grier
Charles Holloway OBE
Linda Keenan
Andrew & Ariana Rodger
Jack Thorne & Rachel Mason
Sandra Treagus for
  ATA Assoc. LTD
Anonymous

Writers' Circle

Chris & Alison Cabot
Cas Donald
Robyn Durie
Héloïse & Duncan Matthews KC
Emma O'Donoghue
Maureen & Tony Wheeler
Anonymous

Directors' Circle

Piers Butler
Fiona Clements
Professor John Collinge
Julian & Ana Garel-Jones
Carol Hall
Dr Timothy Hyde
Anonymous

Platinum Members

Moira Andreae
Tyler Bollier
Katie Bullivant
Anthony Burton CBE
Matthew Dean
Sally & Giles Everist
Emily Fletcher
Beverley Gee
Damien Hyland
Susanne Kapoor
David P Kaskel &
  Christopher A Teano
Peter & Maria Kellner
Robert Ledger &
  Sally Moulsdale
Frances Lynn
Mrs Janet Martin
Andrew McIver
Brian & Meredith Niles
Corinne Rooney
Anita Scott
Bhags Sharma
Dr Wendy Sigle
Brian Smith
Mrs Caroline Thomas
Sir Robert & Lady Wilson
Anonymous

With thanks to our Silver and
Gold Supporters, and our
Friends and Good Friends,
whose support we greatly
appreciate.

Let's be friends. With benefits.

Our Friends and Good Friends are part of the fabric of the Royal Court. They help us to create world-class theatre, and in return they receive early access to our shows and a range of exclusive benefits.

Join today and become a part of our community.

Become a Friend (from £40 a year)

Benefits include:

- Priority Booking
- Advanced access to £15 Monday tickets
- 10% Bar & Kitchen discount (including Court in the Square)
- 10% off Royal Court playtexts

Become a Good Friend (from £95 a year)

In addition to the Friend benefits, our Good Friends also receive:

- Five complimentary playtexts for Royal Court productions
- An invitation for two to step behind the scenes of the Royal Court Theatre at a special event

Our Good Friends' membership also includes a voluntary donation. This extra support goes directly towards supporting our work and future, both on and off stage.

To become a Friend or a Good Friend, or to find out more about the different ways in which you can get involved, visit our website: royalcourttheatre. com/support-us

The English Stage Company at the Royal Court Theatre is a registered charity (No. 231242)

G

Tife Kusoro's work for theatre includes *SW1 Project*, *My White Best Friend (and Other Letters Left Unsaid)*, *Living Newspaper Edition 2* (Royal Court); *We Have Sinned* (45North); *Butterfly* (Talawa). Awards include the George Devine Award (for *G*) and the Royal Court Lynne Gagliano Writers' Award.

TIFE KUSORO

G

faber

First published in 2024
by Faber and Faber Limited
The Bindery, 51 Hatton Garden
London, EC1N 8HN

Typeset by Brighton Gray
Printed and bound in the UK by CPI Group (Ltd), Croydon CR0 4YY

A CIP record for this book
is available from the British Library

ISBN 978-0-571-39251-3

MIX
Paper | Supporting
responsible forestry
FSC® C013604

Printed and bound in the UK on FSC® certified paper in line with our continuing
commitment to ethical business practices, sustainability and the environment.
For further information see faber.co.uk/environmental-policy

2 4 6 8 10 9 7 5 3

Acknowledgements

Thank you, Romana Flello, Vishni Velada-Billson, Ellie Fulcher, Jasmyn Fisher-Ryner, Vicky Berry, for choosing me for Lynne's award.

Thank you, Jane Fallowfield, Nazareth Hassan, Ellie Horne, Gurnesha Bola, Hamish Pirie, Inua Ellams, for all your feedback and guidance.

Thank you, Rory Mullarkey and Sabrina Mahfouz, who led the intro to playwriting group.

Thank you to the first workshop team.

Thank you to the panel of the George Devine Award.

Thank you, David Byrne and Gillian Greer.

Thank you to the team at SISTER pictures.

Thank you to the team at Faber.

Thank you to Jessica Stewart, my agent.

Thank you, Monique, Sel, Ebenezer, Kadiesha, Dani and the entire production team for bringing so much of your light to the play.

Thank you to everyone at the Royal Court.

Thank you to my parents.

Lastly, thank you to Eriife, for coming here with me.

G was first performed at the Royal Court Jerwood Theatre Upstairs, London, on 22 August 2024, with the following cast:

Kai Selorm Adonu
Joy Kadiesha Belgrave
Khaleem Ebenezer Gyau
Baitface Dani Harris-Walters

Director Monique Touko
Designer Madeleine Boyd
Lighting Designer Adam King
Sound Designer Khalil Madovi
Video Designer Tyler Forward
Movement Director & Choreographer Kloé Dean
Costume Designer & Supervisor Rianna Azoro
Casting Director Jatinder Chera
Production Manager Ian Taylor
Stage Manager Nick Graham
Deputy Stage Manager Stacey Nurse

G is a co-production with SISTER.

For my brother, every time

Characters

1

Khaleem
Eighteen. Year 11. Black.
He/him.

Joy
Sixteen. Year 11. Black.
Assigned female at birth but referred
to by the story as he/him.

Kai
Sixteen. Year 11. Black.
Half-brother to Khaleem.
He/him.

0

No_Face
Faceless.
Can't sleep without a pillow.

No_Trace
Faceless.
Terrified of the dark.

No_Case
Faceless.
Afraid of being alone.

Baitface
a god or a ghost or a trick of the light

G

'black boy come like a dark vader'

J Hus

'It is necessary, while in darkness,
to know that there is a light somewhere'

James Baldwin

Notes

1 is the real world and 0 is the world that exists inside a clip of CCTV footage.

THE NIGHT IN QUESTION is the night an alleged 'Crime' took place (these scenes are flashbacks, the rest of the play is in the present).

There are three surveillance cameras pointing towards the exact centre of the stage (these should be placed in or behind the audience and not visible on stage).

A pair of crisp white trainers hang at the exact centre of the stage, right where the cameras point.

1 operates with normal stage lighting.

0 operates with 'night vision' lighting in which each CCTV camera produces a ray of green light through which the audience can see. (This green light is invisible to the characters in this world.)

In 0, the hanging trainers produce white light when polished. This is the only light the characters in this world can see.

Characters should be played in doubles:

Khaleem / No_Face

Joy / No_Trace

Kai / No_Case

In 1, **Baitface** is invisible to the characters.

In 0, he glows with white light.

A bally is whatever a character uses to protect their face.
They can be cartoonish, strange, theatrical, but always a
little uncanny.

– indicates an interruption in speech.

. . . indicates a thought unsaid / a silent response /
a hesitation.

/ indicates where one line overlaps another.

INFLUENCES

Pass Over (play) by Antoinette Nwandu

Big Conspiracy (album) by J Hus

Three brand new, state-of-the-art CCTV cameras.
Their rays point towards the exact centre of the stage.

A pair of crisp white trainers hang, slightly off-centre,
on a power line that crosses above the stage.

Baitface, a masked figure, barefoot, all in white,
enters on a white scooter.

He climbs the wall and slides the hanging trainers
to the point at the centre of the stage;
marking the spot where the cameras point.

THE NIGHT IN QUESTION

It's very late.
Khaleem is walking down a street, alone.

Somewhere else, Kai and Joy are in a bedroom,
sitting cross-legged on the floor opposite each other.
Their shoes are off and placed in between them.
Joy's eyes are closed.
They look like they are meditating,
waiting for something to happen.

Nothing does.

Kai Oi.
Oi.

OI NITTY.
OPEN YOUR EYES.

Joy Maybe if you stop chatting shit you'd feel it.

Kai BRED. Open your eyes and go collect my refund cos
NOTHING'S HAPPENING.

Joy Relax.

Kai How can I relax? This is my life, G. I used my last
money / for this.

Joy Close your eyes and try feel it.

Kai I feel nothing.

Joy WAIT THEN.

> *They wait.*
> *Nothing happens.*

Kai Do you know what's actually supposed to happen?

Joy We wait.

Kai I've BEEN waiting.

Joy We wait for the weed to hit.
And then we wait . . .
. . . to hear his voice or something.

Kai Wait to hear his voice or something???

Joy I don't know.

Kai YOU DON'T KNOW?

Joy NAH BRO. Because not many people have done this
before.
Not many people have been DUMB enough to go under
and get themselves cursed by Baitface.

Kai I'm finished.
I'm actually finished.

Joy Just relax, it'll work.
We'll figure out what to do to reverse the curse.

Kai I still feel nothing.

Joy Wait.

> *It hits.*

Kai Oh shit.
(*Sudden clarity.*) I feel NOTHING.
(*Stroking the air.*) Oh. OHHHH.

> *The bedroom fades into a black void.*
> *Kai and Joy emit light.*

> *Wherever Khaleem is, we see him through*
> *CCTV camera light.*

Has it started? I can feel it.

> *Kai stands up and paces around the void,*
> *looking for something.*
> *He removes his school tie and starts*
> *folding it into a tiny square.*

Joy Sit down. What you doing?

Kai Shh. I need to concentrate.

Joy Sit down.

Kai I need you to protect me.

Joy From what?

Kai I'm unsure of the capacity of my mind at this time.

> *Kai puts his folded tie on the floor.*
> *He takes off his trousers and begins*
> *folding them into a tiny square.*

Joy Kai. What. Are. You. Doing.

Kai I'm not in full control of my mind at this moment in time so I'm getting away from anything that might potentially cause me accidental harm.

Joy Sit down bro. You're fine.

Kai Joy?

Joy Are you gonna sit down?

Kai What if I start screaming for no reason?

Joy What?

Kai Like just for fun. Screaming.
(*Whispering.*) SHIT. WHAT IF I'M SCREAMING RIGHT NOW AND I CAN'T EVEN TELL? Have I been screaming?

Joy Right, you need to pattern cos my neighbour's a snitch and my dad might come back before it wears off.

Kai Okay but promise you'll protect me.

Joy I will protect you. Sit down and close your eyes.

Kai I can't close my eyes what if I fall asleep and then I die?

Joy G. Pattern. You need to sit down if you want it to work.

> *Joy gives Kai his trousers.*
> *Kai puts them on, excruciatingly careful.*

Kai Turn on the light please.

> *Joy flicks a light switch on but we're still in the black.*
> *Kai begins to cry.*

We're trapped.

Joy Remember what I said?

Kai I don't wanna do it any more. I'm scared.

Joy Bro. I'll protect you.

> *Kai nods and sits.*

A looping clip of CCTV footage,
as described below, is played on stage
either as actual camera footage, as performance, or both.

Baitface conceals the faces
of the three figures in the footage.

The Metropolitan Police has obtained CCTV footage that
we understand to show three [

] suspected of A Crime committed against
one Vulnerable Victim in a Borough of London on A Date
Not Too Long Ago. Police are appealing for anyone who
may have information or evidence about the three [
] to come forward.

For more, I'm joined now by our crime correspondent Terry
Davis who is in said Borough of London at The Scene of
The Crime.

Terry what can you tell us about these [

] that we see

captured?

Police are examining the footage as we speak. It's the
first moving footage of our three [
] who appear
close to The Scene of The Crime on The Night in Question.

One of the [   ] was captured by another CCTV camera
alighting the N86 bus on a road close by at 12.47 a.m.,
moments before the footage we see here.

As we see, two of the [   ] appear to engage in some
sort of brief scuffle, while the third . . . well we're not
entirely sure.

But, as we see all three remain remarkably [

].

I

Kai holds his backpack, open,
full to the brim with fresh stock;
brand new ballys in plastic wrapping.

He performs a melodic street cry like
a hawker on a high-street market
or a rapper.

Kai Get you a bally
Don't dilly dally
Baitface is on road
And he ain't your pally

Get you a bally
Don't dilly dally
We've seen what he's like
And he's not after Sally

Get you a bally
Don't dilly dally
One size fits all black boys
Including your daddy

I

London Science Museum, Year 11 trip.
Infrared camera interactive exhibit.

Joy is having a blast, doing some dance moves and
recording himself through the infrared camera projection.

There is only him on stage, but through the projected video
we see that he is surrounded
by a sea of red-hot moving bodies:
museum staff, tourists, the group of girls in his tour group.

Unlike everyone else,
Joy's body on the projection is blue/green.

He doesn't notice this at first, he's just doing his dance.
Then one of the girls comes up beside him
and points out the colour of his body.
Then another one follows, then another,
and another, till a crowd has gathered around him.

Touching him, pointing.
Making red handprints on his face.
Touching him, pointing.

I

Kai and Joy are waiting.
Kai is playing a game with his electric scooter:
he rides around the stage in circles, each round getting
faster and faster, closer and closer to the centre
where the trainers hang.

Joy That's not funny.

Khaleem enters.

Kai Got held in Mr Collins' office late again? He likes you
bares don't he?

Khaleem puts on a bally, climbs the wall and
taps the trainers. When he's done, he takes
the bally off and stays well away from
the trainers.

Khaleem What?

Kai Mr Collins.

Khaleem Oh
yeah yeah
him

> *Kai scoots with no hands. Loses control for a second and gets a bit too close to the centre before he stops.*

Kai HOOOO HOOOO SHIT

Joy You man hear about Daniel?

Kai Which Daniel? There's bare Daniels.
Sosanya
Adekoya
Matimba
Shona
Lomba
Johnson
Bakare
Campbell
Thomas
Anderson
Drummond
. . .
Radcliffe
Craig
Day-Lewis
Kaluuya

Joy Kaluuya. Baitface got Daniel Kaluuya.

> *Kai stops in his tracks.*

Kai Say swear?   **Khaleem** Swear?

Joy SWEAR.

> *They all look up at the hanging trainers in the centre.*

Khaleem Baitface?

Joy Swear. He walked under without covering his face.
Bam. Now watch *Black Panther*.
It's like he was never there.

Kai Mad.

Joy Apparently it makes you forget everything.

Khaleem I heard that too.

Joy And everything forgets you.

Khaleem I heard Jamal from two years above walked
under one of them in Forest Gate without a bally and he
got arrested for robbing a corner shop that he'd never seen
in his life. Now random dogs just bark at him wherever he
goes.

Kai Rah. It got Daniel Kaluuya?
. . . It's survival of the fittest out here.

> *Kai continues his scooter game.*

I

> *Kai and Khaleem.*

Khaleem You got any left?

> *Kai examines Khaleem's old battered bally in his hands.*

Kai Smells like bum crack.

Khaleem How do you know what bum crack smells like?

Kai . . .
Cos of your breath innit.

Khaleem How do you know my breath smells like bum
crack
if you yourself haven't smelled a bum crack first?

Kai Relax with the semantics.
Your breath smells like bum crack,
your bally smells like bum crack.
End of.

Khaleem How much, bro?

> *Kai gets a fresh bally out of his bag.*

Kai Five ninety-nine

Khaleem Five ninety-nine. Yeah?

Kai Yeah yeah

Khaleem No mates' rates?

Kai Nah business is business innit.

Khaleem Calm support Black businesses innit
calm calm

> *Khaleem snatches the bally out of Kai's hand
> and runs.*

1

> *After school.
> Joy and Kai are waiting.*

> *Kai is playing a game with his electric scooter again:
> he accelerates it towards the centre of the stage and
> before he reaches the centre spot where the trainers hang,
> he BRAKES by the skin of his teeth.
> He repositions and does this again
> and again and again.*

Joy Oi, man.
That's not funny.

Kai Nah this is daredevil business.
Harry Houdini and that.
David Blaine and that.

Kai repositions.

Joy Is Khaleem coming?

Kai Late. Got held in Mr Collins' office again.
Bare annoying.
But Mum says I gotta wait with him every day after school
and make sure he's okay.

Joy You know he's lying about Mr Collins giving him
detention . . .

Kai Where is he then?

Joy He joined gospel choir cos he's tryna link Angel.

Kai You're lying.

Joy Don't tell him I told you, he doesn't know I know.

Kai (*bursts out in laughter*) GOSPEL CHOIR?

Joy Mrs Delaney gave him a solo.

Kai NAH.

Joy He's singing 'Shackles' right now.

Kai NAH.

Joy Mary Mary. Yeah. Second verse. The one with the
autotune riff at the end.

Kai CAP.

Joy Don't believe me then.

> *Kai returns his focus to his scooter.*
> *He accelerates towards the centre of the stage.*
> *It's too fast. He can't stop it.*

> *He jumps off to avoid the centre,*
> *just about making it away.*

What the hell man? Be careful.

Kai HOOOOOOO HOOOOOO MY GOD
HOOOOO THAT WAS MAD
HOOOOO J DID YOU SEE THAT?
WHAT DID I SAY?
HARRY FUCKIN HOUDINI

> *Khaleem enters.*
> *Kai and Joy stare at him awkwardly,*
> *like they're hiding something.*

Khaleem What?

> *Khaleem puts on a bally,*
> *climbs the wall and taps the trainers.*

Kai (*staring up at the trainers*) Nah but for real tho, how
do they stay so white?

> *We are transported into:*

○

> *CCTV footage world.*

> *The space is fuelled by a haunting drill melody;*
> *it's as familiar as air to this world.*

> *No_Case stands on a wall,*
> *polishing the hanging trainers to produce light.*
> *No_Face is fast asleep, using No_Trace*
> *(who is also asleep) as a pillow.*

> *(No_Case, No_Face and No_Trace*
> *are the figures in the CCTV come to life.)*

No_Case Oi.
Oi.
Oiiiiii man.
Wake up.
Your shift.
Oi.

>   *He slides his shoe off with his foot*
>   *and drops it on No_Face.*

No_Face (*in sleep*) Shh, man. Lemme concentrate.

No_Case You've been concentrating for time, G.

>   *He drops his other shoe, harder.*
>   *Silence. Sleep.*
>   *He stops polishing.*
>   *The trainer light quickly dims to complete blackness.*

No_Trace (*waking, hysterical*) WHAT THE FUCK, MAN.
POLISH THE TING. / POLISH THE TING. DON'T PLAY.

No_Face Wasteman. I was having a DREAM as well.

>   *No_Case resumes polishing.*
>   *The trainer light brightens.*

No_Trace Don't play with that shit.

No_Face Why you gonna wake me from MY DREAM,
man.

No_Case Your. Shift.

No_Face I said I was dreaming, G. DREAMING.

No_Case What you got to dream about?

No_Face . . .
Bare tings.

No_Case Well dream that you're AWAKE and on your
SHIFT, G.

31

No_Face Relax.

No_Case I should relax?

No_Face Relax.

No_Case You want me to relax?

No_Face Relax yourself, G.

> *No_Case relaxes, drops his arms, stops polishing.*
> *The trainer light dims to black.*

No_Trace WHAT DID I SAY? DON'T PLAY.
DON'T PLAY THESE / GAMES WITH MY HEART.

No_Face OKAY. ALRIGHT. Fine.

> *No_Case resumes polishing.*

Childish.

> *No_Face gets up, sluggish.*

No_Trace Swiftness, man.

No_Face I know, G. Untwist your knickers.

> *No_Face picks up No_Case's shoes and,*
> *when he can't see,*
> *rubs them in his bum crack.*

> *No_Face offers shoes to No_Case.*

Special delivery for you my G.

> *No_Case drapes the polish cloth over the hanging trainers*
> *so that the light dims significantly slower.*
> *He climbs down the wall and puts on his shoes.*

> *No_Face climbs up and begins to polish lazily,*
> *the light is only semi-bright.*

No_Case Ay, you man. Don't today sound different to you?

No_Trace Different how?

No_Case Nah listen listen listen

No_Trace (*listening*) I don't hear nothing different.

No_Case Nah you gotta listen with your eyes closed
so your ears got more precision, G
listen

No_Trace (*listening harder with eyes closed*) Nah, sounds
the same as yesterday, G.

> *No_Case stands real close to No_Trace.*

No_Case Nah listen listen listen it's there
it's in the hi-hat listen
ss ss ss

ss ss ss

ss ss ss

~sscared of the dark pussy wasteman neek~
RAHHHHHHHHHHH YOU HEAR THAT? mad

> *No_Face bursts into laughter.*
> *He loses focus on polishing and the light begins to dim.*

No_Trace rahhhhhhhhhhhhhhh you got jokes.

No_Case Nah nah nah nah it's not me bro.
Just bare subliminals in the ting.
Illuminati and dem man.

No_Face How do you let him get you EVERY SINGLE
DAY, G?

No_Trace HoW Do YoU lEt HiM gEt YoU EvErY sInGlE
dAy G?
Mind your business and revert your focus to your shift,
G.

> *No_Face resumes polishing, light brightens.*

No_Face Aight den
. . .
scared of the dark pussy wasteman neek

No_Trace Come ask me to be your pillow next time you wanna sleep you paigon.

No_Face Aight sorry sorry sorry sorry sorry sorry sorry sorry

> *The background melody kicks into a beat.*
>
> *No_Case and No_Trace slip almost unnoticeably into a looping movement with each other: somewhere between a rough dance and an altercation.*
> *Somehow even they don't notice.*

Oi
Do you man wanna hear my dream?

No_Case Nah.   **No_Trace** Nope.

No_Face Aight so boom
I'm sleeping yeah
and then I just see this
this this this this naaah
this this this this this / this this

No_Case (*to No_Trace*) Here we go again with the light, bro.

No_Face THIS LIGHT.

No_Trace Yeah you saw the light bruv
this is a recurring dream.

No_Face Recurring what's that?

No_Trace Means we heard it bare times, G.

No_Face Nah nah nah not even.
This light in this dream weren't just any light
it weren't no shoe-polish light
it was it was it was it was / the proper light

No_Case proper light   **No_Trace** proper light

No_Trace Tell me one thing
how did you see this light
when you're sleeping and your eyes are closed

No_Face That's what I mean, G.
It weren't none of this this this –

No_Case This shit.

No_Face THIS SHIT.
I'm telling you there was bare rays
like BAAAAAARE
like blinding
like penetrating the eyelids, G.

No_Case Errrrrrr man. Allow it.

No_Face NAH
like penetrating the third eye, G.
This shit I dreamt about bro
This LIGHT
yoooooooooooooooooooooo
iss the shit we've been waiting for
there was no more shifts and that
no rotation just relaxation
inna sunshine vacation
three of us just there
just there shining
just shining like a bald man's head

> *No_Trace quietly ad libs à la DJ Khaled*
> *ft. Beyonce & Jay Z's 'Shining'.*

No_Trace shining shining shining shining yeah

No_Case Bare exposed
bare asking to be slapped yeah

No_Face EXACTLY
bare glowing
bare vivid and that

and then I felt this feeling
this feeling
this this this this this this / seen feeling –

No_Trace Yeah seeing feeling yeah we heard this

No_Face Nah nah nah SEEN feeling

No_Trace You what mate?

No_Face Like
(*Patois.*) *seen.*

No_Case Oh
(*Patois.*) *seen.*

No_Trace OHHHHHH
(*Patois.*) *seen.*

No_Face YES, G.

No_Trace Yeah
. . .
. . .
. . .
yeah nah not gonna lie you deffo had this dream yesterday /
still

No_Face Oi shutup bruv.

o.

No_Trace is polishing the trainer light.
He plays a game with No_Case to keep occupied.

No_Face is trying to sleep but can't.

No_Trace Gander.

No_Case Guatemala.

No_Trace Gully.

No_Case Goop.

No_Face Not a real word.

No_Case Your face is not a real word.

No_Trace Glass.

No_Case Grenade.

No_Face You said that two hundred and four words ago.

No_Case GrenadeS.

No_Face You banned plurals when you were on C.

No_Case Bro.
You're not playing.

No_Face Can't sleep.

No_Case If you're not playing, shut up.

No_Face Just saying. Your rules.

Beat.

No_Case Goat.

No_Face Gremlin.

No_Case Gorilla.

No_Face Gargantuan germ.

No_Case Godforsaken goblin.

No_Face Goddamned gazebo-head.

No_Case Gazebo-head?

No_Trace Yeah that was weak, still.

No_Case Geriatric goose.

No_Trace Gangrene-ridden gargoyle.

No_Case . . .

No_Face . . .

No_Trace Gentrified grasshopper.
Giraffe-necked gingerbread man.
Glorified grain of garri.

> *No_Face takes off his shoe and throws it at No_Trace.*

○

> *No_Trace polishes the trainer light.*
>
> *No_Face, still unable to sleep,
> has taken off layers of his clothing
> and tucked them to make himself a pillow.*
>
> *No_Case is flipping through a homework diary.*

No_Case Listen to this listen to this listen to this

No_Face Not again.

No_Case (*raps from diary.*) Slide in like a secret samuraaaai
step too close and I'll bleed your bruddas dryyyy
sword sharp
but I move in silence
no sirens
no sirens
nice and quiet
simple science
stay slick and
rob this island
mask on no fuckin alibiiiiiiii

No_Trace It's my turn.

No_Case I'm not done yet.

No_Trace You've had ages, man.

No_Case And I'm not done.

No_Trace Awww allow it, man. My arms hurt.

No_Case Peak.

No_Trace Paigon.

No_Case Nah nah noway hosay. What are the golden rules?

No_Trace . . .

No_Case Page thirty-two.

> *No_Case flips to page 32 of the homework diary.*
> *Holds up the page of golden rules.*

No_Case Golden rule number three:
We are polite and have good manners.
Golden rule number four:
We will treat our brethren with respect.

No_Trace Fine. You've got five minutes.

> *Beat.*

No_Case Aight listen to this listen to this listen to this

No_Face Please no.

No_Trace Do the sweet one.

No_Case Which one?

No_Trace The one about the Angel.

No_Case That one's dead.

No_Trace I wanna hear it.

No_Case Nah.

No_Trace Please, man.

No_Case flips to a new page in the homework diary.

No_Case Aight listen to this listen to this listen to this

I said
wagwarn bebé
can't ya
tell dat I'm crazé
ya said I'm
makin ya hate mé
but I been
missin ya latelé

can't ya see I'm going cou cou
yeah ya
twisted ma loose screw
girl are ya
carrying ju ju
cos the way dat I need you

I said
come close Angel
neva been
unfaithful
ask me what I bring to da table
I'll tell ya
go ask Rachel

lock off ma heart make the key go
missin
mek I give you some chocolate
kissin
bring your lips close an' talk
lemme listen
baby
say how you're feelin
(*etc.*)

No_Trace Cold.
Chilly con carne.

No_Case Aight listen to this listen to this / listen to this

No_Face NO

No_Trace It's my turn it's my turn man

> *They switch places.*
> *No_Case polishes.*
> *No_Trace flips through the diary.*
> *No_Face still can't sleep.*

No_Face (*to No_Trace*) Please please please please just for a bit
just for a bit

No_Trace . . .

No_Case (*to No_Trace*) Listen to me. Don't let the devil rule you. What's golden rule number five?

No_Trace (*reads aloud from the homework diary*) We will participate with / effort and enthusiasm.

No_Case WE WILL PARTICIPATE WITH EFFORT AND ENTHUSIASM.
Now, is this bredda showing effort or enthusiasm?

No_Trace Nah.

No_Case So don't let him use you.

No_Face Aww allow it I just wanna sleep.

No_Trace I can't be your pillow I'm busy.

No_Case (*to No_Trace*) Good man.
(*To No_Face.*) It's not me, it's the golden rules, bro.

No_Face As established by who?

No_Case The book, G.
Read it.

No_Trace Aight listen to this listen to this listen to this

No_Face Not again.

The background melody kicks into a beat
No_Trace drops the diary and begins to
slip into the looping movement with No_Face.

I

Kai and Joy stare at the hanging trainers on the wire above.

Kai Did they say whose homework diary it was?

Joy Nah.

Kai But it was definitely one of George Grierson Academy?

Joy Yeah.

Kai Mad.

Joy What's gonna happen?

Kai Dunno.

. . .

How many are they looking for?

Joy Three.

Kai Bait?

Joy Nah they didn't get their faces.

> *Kai scrambles for something in his bag.*
> *His homework diary.*
> *He drops it on the floor.*

Kai I've got mine.

Joy So you're fine.

Kai I got a warning.

Joy You?

Kai From Mr Tomlin. First one since Year Seven.

Joy Rah.

Kai Chantelle told the nurse my chicken mayo salad wrap gave her diarrhoea.

Joy Your chicken mayo salad wraps are elite.

Kai That's what I told Mr Tomlin. No sir, it didn't, cos my chicken mayo salad wraps are elite. Chantelle's chatting more shit than what's coming out her arse.

Joy What he say?

Kai What a way to represent the school, Kai.
Selling food illegally to your fellow students.
This is not what I expected of you as head boy, Kai.
I'm giving you a red warning.

Joy Not even amber?

Kai That's what I said.
I said not even amber?
He said, your offence is too great for an amber warning, Kai.
And then he confiscated my whip.

Joy No.

Kai Can't get her back till the end of term.
. . .
There's no way it was one of my chicken mayo salad wraps.

Joy You think it's cos of Baitface?

Kai Why else?

Joy I thought we reversed it that night?

Kai Well there's no way it was one of my chicken mayo salad wraps.

Joy is alone.

He looks around to make sure no one is watching, then he puts his hood up and pulls the drawstrings so the hood tightens around his face till it can no longer be seen.

Then he climbs the wall, taps the trainers, gets back down, untightens his hoodie, and checks around to make absolutely sure that no one saw him.

I

Kai, Khaleem and Joy are waiting.

Joy and Kai are rapping over a drill instrumental on a phone. Khaleem is somewhere else, occupied with his phone.

Kai Bro bro's got a hammer

Joy That's why we call him Thor

Kai Please don't make him rise his tool

They wait for Khaleem to pick up the next line but he is completely occupied with his phone, giggling like a fool.

Please don't make him rise his tool . . .

Joy Khaleem

Khaleem What, man?

Kai The line.

Khaleem Oh, you man are bare childish.

Khaleem goes back to giggling on his phone.

Joy He's texting Angel again, fuck's sake.

Kai (*throws his shoe at Khaleem*) Get your priorities straight, man.

Joy What so are you linking her now?

Khaleem Mind your business.

Kai Aww did you guys kissy wissy on the bus that night?

Khaleem SHUT UP BRUV.

> *Khaleem continues giggling on his phone.*

I

> *Joy is staring at the trainers on the wire.*

> *Kai and Khaleem are mid-scuffle.*
> *Kai is struggling onto Khaleem, trying to get into his*
> *backpack.*

Khaleem Get off me, man!

Kai Show me.

Khaleem No!

Kai Come on.

Khaleem Move, man!

Kai I just wanna know it's there.

Khaleem Get off. What's your business?

Kai I just need to.

Khaleem WHY?

Kai BECAUSE.

Khaleem BECAUSE WHAT? Get the fuck off me, man!

Khaleem gets Kai off him with force.
Kai falls on the floor.

Beat.

Joy Police found a homework diary.
They're saying whoever's it is might be involved with The Crime on the news.

They all look up at the hanging trainers.

Then Baitface appears.
He's up there with the trainers.
A god or a ghost or a trick of the light.
The boys can't see him.

Kai Something's wrong.

I

Still up there, Baitface watches:
Khaleem is alone.

He puts on a bally, climbs the wall
and pulls the hanging trainers down.
He makes sure no one is watching him,
then he stuffs the trainers in his bag.
When the trainers are in and the
bag is zipped, he takes off the bally and
exits by crossing the centre of the stage
where the CCTV cameras point.

Then the space flashes into negative.

A name is captured and projected
like computer code in a database:
KHALEEM TIJAN JAWARA

*

Joy enters. Sees the empty space on the wire.
In quiet disbelief he gets closer
and looks up at it from underneath.
He exits.

Then the space flashes into negative.

Another name is captured and projected:
JOY ALIYAH CLARKE
He exits.

*

Kai enters. Sees the empty space on the wire.
He looks around to see if it's a prank. Then rides his scooter
right up underneath it to see that it's real. It is.
He exits.

Then the space flashes into negative.

Another name is captured and projected:
KAI JOSEPH OKAFOR

*

Then a multitude of NAMES.
(Maybe the full names of some well known Black men.)

Then all the names turn into 1s and 0s.
1s and 0s everywhere.

Baitface exits.

o

The trainer light is gone.
We see them through the light of the surveillance cameras
but they can't see each other.
The drill bassline is thicker, scarier, mad.

No_Case and No_Face are stuck
in the looping movement with each other.
It isn't like before; it is heavier, darker.
They don't need to be able to see to do it.

No_Trace is terrified.

No_Trace nah nah nah nah nah nah nah nah nah nah nah
nah nah nah nah nah nah nah nah nah nah nah nah nah
nah nah nah nah nah nah nah nah nah nah nah nah nah
nah nah nah nah nah nah nah YOU MAN
nah nah nah nah nah nah nah nah nah nah nah nah nah
nah nah nah nah nah nah nah nah nah nah nah nah nah
nah nah nah nah nah nah nah nah nah nah nah nah nah
nah nah nah nah nah YOU MAN STOP
STOP

o

Still darkness.
We can still see through the camera light.

No_Case and No_Face are
still stuck in the looping movement.

No_Trace nah nah nah nah nah nah nah nah nah nah nah
nah nah nah nah nah nah nah nah nah nah NAH NAH NAH
NAH NAH NAH NAH NAH NAH NAH NAH NAH NAH
NAH NAH NAH NAH NAH NAH NAH NAH NAH NAH
NAH NAH NAH NAH NAH NAH NAH NAH NAH NAH

NAH NAH NAH NAH NAH NAH NAH NAH NAH NAH
NAH NAH NAH NAH NAH NAH NAH NAH NAH NAH
NAH NAH NAH NAH NAH NAH NAH NAH NAH NAH
NAH NAH NAH NAH NAH

o

> *Still darkness.*
> *No_Case and No_Face are*
> *still stuck in the looping movement.*

No_Trace is sat on the floor rocking, hyperventilating.

I

Kai Just show me your diary.

> *Khaleem puts on his bally and goes through his bag.*
> *He gets out the white trainers and drops them*
> *on the floor next to Kai's homework diary.*

Khaleem It's fine.

Kai . . .

Joy . . .

Kai . . .

. . .
yo what the fuck, man?

Joy You took them down?

Khaleem Yeah.

Joy No one's ever taken them down.

o

Still darkness.
No_Case and No_Face are
still stuck in the looping movement.

No_Trace is still sat on the floor rocking, hyperventilating.

I

Kai ANGEL. WE ARE ALL FINISHED COS YOU'RE
TRYNA MOVE ANGEL?

Joy mumbles this throughout the entire scene, hysterical.

Joy nah nah nah nah nah nah nah nah nah nah nah nah
nah nah nah nah nah nah nah nah nah nah nah nah
nah nah nah nah nah nah nah nah nah nah nah nah
nah nah nah nah nah nah

Khaleem No one's finished.

Kai So why did I get a red warning?

Khaleem Look at my face. I'm covered.
I've been covered the whole time I've had them.
Covered when I took them down.
Covered when I put them in my bag.
Covered when I took them out.
I'm fine.

Kai I got a RED warning. RED. NOT EVEN AMBER.
My whole hustle is in jeopardy.
Tomlin took my business vehicle.

Khaleem It's a fuckin e-scooter.

Kai You took the trainers down to impress some –

Khaleem Angel. She wanted to see them innit. I told her they've been up there for twenty years and there ain't a speck of dust on them and she said she wanted to see.

Kai So you took them down. And now SOMETHING is wrong.

Khaleem Nothing's wrong.

Kai Show me your diary then.

Khaleem Move.

Kai I asked every single black boy from Year Seven to Eleven to show me their diary and they did.
Except Abraham.

Khaleem So go ask Abraham.

Kai Abraham is sick at home and he still snapped me a picture of his diary.
Everyone's accounted for except you.

Khaleem Untwist your knickers, golden boy.

Kai Show me your diary.

> *Khaleem ties the laces of the white trainers back together.*
> *He climbs the wall and hangs them*
> *back up in their exact position.*

Khaleem Fixed.

Kai Not fixed until you show me your diary.

> *Khaleem takes everything out of his backpack.*
> *One dog-eared exercise book.*
> *One single pen.*

Is there nothing else?

> *Khaleem scrapes the bottom of his bag and brings out*
> *a handful of pencil shavings that he sprinkles*
> *slowly onto the ground.*

. . .
you don't have it.

Khaleem Clearly not.

Kai Where is it?

Khaleem [*How am I supposed to know?*]

Kai If this doesn't fix up, I'm not going down with you.
You're not gonna take me where you're going.

o

> *The trainer light is back.*
> *The bassline has calmed down.*
> *Everything is as it previously was.*
>
> *No_Case is polishing the trainer light.*
> *No_Trace is trying to sleep.*
>
> *No_Face is staring at the audience.*
> *He takes his mask off and underneath it he is faceless.*
> *He takes the next mask off and it's the same.*
> *And the next the same. And the next.*
> *He repeats this throughout the scene*
> *always looking out suspiciously,*
> *wondering what is there and*
> *if they can see.*

No_Case Oi.
Oi.
Oiiiiii man.
Wake up.
Your shift.
Oi.

> *He slides his shoe off and drops it on No_Face.*

No_Face Shh, man. Can't you see that I'm awake?

No_Case Oh shit, yeah.
My bad.

No_Face Lemme concentrate.

No_Case You've been concentrating for time, G.
(*Seeing No_Face taking off his ?face?*) Errrrr man. Stop
doing that.

No_Face Why?

No_Case Cos it's disgusting.

> *Beat.*

YOUR SHIFT.

No_Face Wait.
Stop that for a sec.

No_Case You what mate?

No_Face Stop doing that for a sec.

No_Case Why?

No_Face Just for a sec. I wanna see something.

No_Case What about –

No_Face Relax he's asleep.

No_Case Nah, bro.

No_Face Stop doing it for a sec and I'll switch.

> *No_Case slows down his polishing.*
> *The light goes out.*
>
> *No_Face looks out, suspiciously.*
> *He does something dramatic to provoke a reaction.*
> *Even if there is a reaction, he can't see it.*

No_Trace (*waking in the darkness*) NAH. YOU MAN ARE MOCKING IT.
I'VE HAD ENOUGH.

No_Case resumes polishing.

No_Case He told me to do it.
Sorry.

No_Trace Nah. Some changes gotta be made round here cos you man are mocking it.

No_Face Ay, when did we meet?

No_Trace . . .

No_Case . . .

No_Face Nah serious
us three when did we meet?

No_Case Time ago.

No_Face How long we been here?

No_Trace For time.

No_Face How much?

No_Case Bare.

No_Face How much time is bare?

No_Trace Bare / time.

No_Case Bare time is bare time innit.
Bare.

No_Face And where are we?

No_Trace . . .

No_Case . . .

No_Trace Aight.
Your turn.
Why are you a lazy fucking wasteman?

No_Face . . .

No_Trace Question time innit.
Why is your head like that?

No_Face Like what?

No_Case Nah nah nah
He's right. Still.
Your head is like –

No_Face Shutup bruv.

No_Case Oi.
Oi.
Oiiiiii man.
Switch.
Your shift.

No_Face . . .

Beat.

No_Case Ay, you man.
Don't today sound different to you.

No_Trace Different how?

No_Case Nah listen listen listen

No_Trace I don't hear nothing different.

No_Case Nah you gotta listen with your eyes closed
so your ears got more precision, G
listen

No_Trace (*listening harder with eyes closed*) Nah, sounds
the same as yesterday, G.

No_Case Nah listen listen listen it's there
it's in the hi-hat listen
ss ss ss
ss ss ss
ss ss ss

~sscared of the dark pussy wasteman neek~
RAHHHHHHHHHHHH YOU HEAR THAT? mad

No_Trace Rahhhhhhhhhhhhhhh you got jokes.

No_Case Nah nah nah nah it's not me bro.
Just bare subliminals in the ting.
Illuminati and dem man.

No_Face how do you let him get you every single day, G

No_Trace HoW Do YoU lEt HiM gEt YoU EvErY sInGlE

dAy, G?

> *The background melody kicks into a beat.*

> *No_Trace slips almost unnoticeably*
> *into the looping movement.*
> *No_Face doesn't.*

Oi
Do you man wanna hear my dream?

No_Case Nah.   **No_Trace** Nope.

No_Face . . .
. . .
. . .
forget it.

No_Case (*to No_Trace*) Here we go again with the light,
bro.

No_Trace Yeah nah not gonna lie you deffo had this dream
yesterday /
still

> *Baitface takes the mask off No_Face*
> *revealing Khaleem's face.*

The Metropolitan Police have obtained new evidence
following The Crime that took place in One Borough of
London
on A Night Not Too Long Ago.

> The homework diary of eighteen-year-old KHALEEM
> JAWARA, a Year Eleven student of George Grierson
> Academy has been found close to The Scene of The Crime.

> He is believed to be the figure that alighted the N86 bus on
> a road close by at 12.47 a.m. That Night.

Pages of the diary contain what appear to be lyrics
promoting knife crime, robbery and violence against police
and local authority.

THE NIGHT IN QUESTION (CONTINUED)

> *Kai and Joy emit light.*
> *Khaleem is somewhere else, alone, walking.*
> *We see him through CCTV light.*

Kai We're trapped.

Joy Remember what I said?

Kai I don't wanna do it any more. I'm scared.

Joy Bro. I'll protect you.

> *Kai nods and sits.*

(*Handing him a bally.*) Aight, you have to put it on now. To be safe.

Kai In case anything happens to me
I need to tell you something

Joy Nothing's gonna happen to you.

Kai I just need to tell you something

Joy Stop being weird and just put it on.

> *Kai puts on the bally.*
> *They wait.*

Kai Please God let it work please God let it work please God let it work please God let it work please God –

> *Beat.*

Kai Wait. Did you hear that?

Joy What?

Kai I sound like Khaleem.

Joy . . .

Kai Ohmygod CAN YOU HEAR THAT
????????????????????

Joy Kai. Please focus.

Kai No. This isn't my voice. Yooooooo. I sound exactly like Khaleem.

Joy Yeah, if Khaleem sounded exactly like you.

Kai Is this what's supposed to happen?

Joy No.

Kai I can see him without seeing him like I can feel what he's feeling.

> *Kai gets up and starts pacing around the void again.*

Do you think it's cos we've got the same DNA?

Joy KAI. If you want it to work, sit down.

Kai Shhhh. Let me concentrate.

> *Beat.*

He's eating wings, I can taste it.

Joy You can taste wings.

Kai (*tasting his own mouth*) This is MAAAAD.

> *Kai begins to walk in exaggerated*
> *slow motion, on one spot.*
> *He matches Khaleem's movements precisely;*
> *eating wings.*

Joy You're acting long. Kai. Sit down.

Kai I swear this isn't me. It's Khaleem.

Joy So, your brother is walking with your legs.

Kai Joy. I'm serious.
I can feel the wings sliding down my guy's throat.

> *Kai mimes finishing the chicken, licking his fingers,*
> *emptying the bones in a bin. Then, weirdly*
> *folding the cardboard box.*

Joy What are you doing?

Kai I think he's recycling the chicken box.

> *He mimes putting the folded cardboard in a separate bin.*

Knew he was a neek.

Joy You serious that you can feel him?

Kai Mad serious cuz.

> *Kai continues to walk.*
> *He fidgets with something invisible on his wrist;*
> *Khaleem fidgets with a beaded bracelet on his wrist.*

Joy What's that what's that what is it?

Kai Dunno. Feels nice.

Kai and Khaleem slow down.

Joy What's he doing now?

Kai Wait. Wait.

. . .

. . .

bus stop.

Kai and Khaleem both lean on an invisible bus-stop bench.

Joy What now?

Kai . . .

Joy . . .

Kai begins to cry;
Khaleem doesn't, he puts on his bally.

What what what what what

Kai I don't know. It's not me, is it.

Kai clings to the invisible thing on his wrist;
Khaleem clings to the beaded bracelet on his wrist.

We gotta go find him.

Kai rushes off.

Joy Kai, wait.
Where?

Kai The spot.
Near the bus stop on Romford Road!

Joy grabs their shoes and follows.

Khaleem and Joy.

Khaleem It was like *CSI*.
. . .
Nah. *Criminal Minds*.

Joy Lies.

Khaleem Swear down.
They had that one invisible window that looks like a mirror
where they can watch you but you don't know they're
watching you cos you can only see yourself.
But obviously man knew they were watching me innit.
One naked eye-looking light bulb bare swinging from the
ceiling like in them films. Tape recorder, everything.

Joy What did they ask?

Khaleem Bare tings.
Where was I on The Night in Question why was my
homework diary there et cetera et cetera

Joy What did you say?

Khaleem Said I don't know innit
don't remember.

Joy You don't?

Khaleem Can't remember one thing. It's mad.

Joy So they gave it back?

Khaleem Nah. They're keeping it as evidence. And they've
got the audacity to think that I'm a thief?
I'm just minding my business trying to complete my
education and they take my homework diary away to dust
it off with their forensics like it's a strap.
Tell me how'm I supposed to do my homework now?

Joy You ain't done homework since September, bro.

Khaleem Oi shutup bruv.

I

Kai, Khaleem and Joy are waiting.

Khaleem Grandma.

Kai God.

Joy Goddess.

Khaleem Goggles.

Kai Government.

Joy Glove.

Khaleem G-string.

He giggles.

Kai Childish.

Khaleem *You're* childish.

Kai Galloping gecko.

Khaleem Goliath of a guinea pig.

Kai Gallivanting gynaecologist.

Khaleem Giant gnat.

Kai Global piece of garbage.

Khaleem Gold-plated garden gnome.

Kai Ga . . . Ga . . .

Joy whispers a cheat in Kai's ear.

(*To Joy.*) Come again?

Khaleem Nah! You can't do that!

Kai Gastrointestinal granuloma.

> *Joy gives him another one.*

Galactic glioblastoma.

I

> *Joy and Khaleem are waiting.*
>
> *Joy is running up and down the walls,
> somersaulting, and jumping over
> Khaleem who is mumbling lines to himself
> and writing them into a notebook.*

Khaleem Listen. Bro.
If you kick my head I will kick your head.

Joy Do you think it's gonna be weird?

Khaleem It's already weird bruv.

Joy Nah but, do you think it'll be weird if I join?

Khaleem You *are* weird, bruv.

Joy Yeah but not like weird, right?

Khaleem Listen. Do your ting.
If you join there's less chance of you kicking my head.
And therefore less chance of me kicking your head.
Win win.

Joy But with all the boys, it's not weird?
Mr Reed said yeah but my dad thinks it's weird.

Khaleem It's not.

Joy I guess it'll be like you being in gospel choir.

Khaleem . . .
I'm not in gospel choir.

Joy . . .
yeah . . . okay . . .

> *Joy continues his acrobatics.*
> *He teases Khaleem by quietly singing*
> *'Shackles' by Mary Mary.*

Khaleem I will kick your head.

> *Joy does a run up the wall.*
> *His shadow against the wall is suddenly MASSIVE.*
> *It terrifies him. He drops mid-run.*

Khaleem You okay?

Joy Yeah yeah yeah nah nah nah it's nothing I'm good I'm calm

> *He is not good. He is not calm.*

1

> *A shop.*

> *Joy carries two grocery bags full to the*
> *brim with food and household stuff.*
> *He steps out through the security system.*
> *Alarm goes off.*

> *He steps back in.*
> *Drops the bags.*
> *Steps out.*
> *Security alarm goes off.*

He steps back in.
Removes his belt and watch.
Puts down his phone.
Steps out.
Security alarm goes off.

He steps back in.
Takes off his earrings and crucifix.
Steps out.
Security alarm goes off.

He steps back in.
Takes off his shoes and jacket.
Steps out.
Security alarm goes off.

He steps back in.
Empties his pockets;
1. Handful of copper coins.
2. Inhaler.
3. Beyblade.
Steps out.
Security alarm goes off.

He steps back in.
Takes off his shirt and trousers.
Steps out in his vest and boxers.
Security alarm goes off.

He steps back in.
Tries again.
Steps out in his vest and boxers.
Security alarm goes off.

He steps back in.

Kai, Khaleem and Joy are waiting.

Kai polishes his scooter rigorously.

Khaleem looks like shit, like he hasn't slept in days.
He has dozed off, using his bally as an eye-mask.

Joy occasionally rubs his ear
with his hand, violently, like he is
trying to get a sound out.

Joy You man ever feel like you're being followed?

Kai . . .
What like in Sainsbury's Local?
Get used to it.

Joy Nah like being watched.

Kai Okay.
One. If you feel like it's God
You're right.
Go confession.

Two. If you feel like it's MI6
Option A: put tape on your camera.
Option B: private browser slash VPN.
Option C: clear your search history every two hours.
Same conditions apply if you feel like it's your mum.

Joy . . .

Kai Shit sorry I didn't mean to –

Joy Nah I mean like,
you man ever feel like you're being collected?

Kai . . .

. . .
Think your cousin's been letting you smoke too much weed,
bro
drink some water.

> *Kai is struggling to scrape a red*
> *'CONFISCATED ITEM' sticker off his scooter.*

FUCKSAKE.

Joy You should take it back before they find out.

Kai It's my property.

Joy Your dad bought it innit?

Kai . . .

. . .

you got any nail-varnish remover?

Joy Why would I have nail-varnish remover?

Kai Dunno. Thought you might innit.
(*To Khaleem, who is twitching, mumbling in his sleep.*) Oi.
Oi.
Oiiiii man.
WAKE UP.

> *Khaleem shoots awake like he's just been*
> *pulled out of the ocean or something.*

Khaleem (*panicking, trying to get his bally off*) Angel angel
angel angel where's my face my face my face my face bro
where's my face nah my face my face

Kai G
You good?

Khaleem Nah.
That FUCKING dream.

I

> *Joy is alone.*
> *The security alarm rings like tinnitus in his ears.*
> *Louder and louder and louder and louder.*

He rubs his ears to make it stop.
It doesn't.

Kai is alone.
Looking everywhere for his scooter.
It is nowhere to be found.

Khaleem is alone.
He is trying to sleep but tossing
turning twitching mumbling.

I

Kai, Khaleem and Joy are waiting.

Kai He's gonna kill me he's gonna kill me he's gonna kill me he's gonna kill me he's gonna kill me

Joy Who?

Khaleem Me, if you don't shutup.

Kai My dad he's gonna kill me he's gonna kill me

Joy Why?

Kai I can't find it I parked it I parked it behind the bush at back gate before school and now it's not there no more he's gonna kill me

Khaleem Not this fucking scooter again.

Kai It was there I parked it there this morning so Mr Tomlin wouldn't see that I took it back and now it's not there no more

Joy Okay okay relax.

Kai I went Bilal's to ask him to check his cameras outside to see who took it and he said he couldn't he couldn't he said he said he said

Joy Kai, bro, bro, bro, calm down

Kai He said he said who are you I've never seen you round here before can't just come in here telling me to check my cameras

Joy Bossman Bilal?

Kai I said I said Bilal it's me I come here every breaktime eleven a.m. Bilal come on I came in here yesterday I come in here everyday and I buy sixteen cans of KA four black grape four fruit punch four kola four pineapple Bilal Billy the bossman it's me it's me you know me you know my name people say my name at the counter to get twenty P off number two please Bilal just check your cameras someone's jacked my scooter my dad's gonna kill me he said he said he said he said what's your name

. . .

. . .

. . .

. . .

Joy Yeah?

Kai He said what's your name then tell me your name and I

. . .

. . .

. . .

you know my name Billyman I just need to know who took my scooter
I know my name

Joy Kai.

Kai Yes. Kai Kai fucking Kai but I couldn't say it could I I couldn't say it like my mind just went blank like black like nothing like I couldn't remember. Kai.

K-A-I. Kai. Fucking Kai. One syllable.
KAI KAI KAI KAI KAI KAI KAI KAI KAI KAI

Joy You can still find it.

Kai I couldn't say it just ran out of the shop and I still
dunno who took it he's gonna kill me he's gonna kill me if
I don't get it back he's gonna kill me

Khaleem It's a scooter bruv you're not gonna die
your dad is rich.

Kai YOU DON'T KNOW
you don't know what's gonna –

I

Kai and Khaleem are waiting.

Khaleem She blocked me.

Kai Who?

Khaleem Angel.
Angel blocked me. She won't talk to me no more.

Kai Oh.
Nah nah nah that's normal. It's called the ick.
She probably started to notice the eczema around your nose
a bit too much.

Khaleem No. You spoke to her and now she won't talk to
me no more.

Kai Ohhhh that. Is that it? That's calm.

Khaleem Keep my name out your mouth.

Kai She asked me innit. Didn't wanna lie.

Khaleem Keep it out your mouth.

Kai It's not like it's a secret.
It's public knowledge innit word's already on road relax
all I did was tell her what everyone already knows.

Khaleem It's not true.

Kai You should be thanking me, bro. All these females
want is two things:
One: honesty.
Two: a cheeky Nando's every non-uniform day.
I just gave you half of that. You're welcome.

Khaleem Tell her it's not true.

Kai She asked me how come you're eighteen and still in
Year Eleven
and I told her its cos you got kicked out of your old school
for beating up the head of year.
Everyone knows.

Khaleem THAT'S NOT WHAT HAPPENED.

Kai Okay.

> *Joy enters, wearing a school skirt*
> *instead of the usual trousers.*

> *Kai takes it in for a beat*
> *then bursts into hysterics.*

YO WHY CAN I SEE YOUR LEGS BRUV?

Joy Shutup. My dad's making me wear it.

Kai Nah nah nah nah nah
you look like
you look like
. . .
ay yo B lemme chat to you real quick.

Joy Just shutup and let's go.

Kai You feeling the breeze yeah?

Joy He said it's safer. Shutup.

Kai Coming like a Scotsman /
oh wait nah Scotswoman.

Joy Shutup.

Kai Nah . . . wait . . . nah I take that one back that one
don't work.

Joy Let's go.

Kai Think you gotta walk behind us today so Khaleem
doesn't start catching feelings.

Khaleem Shutup, man.

Kai Nah nah nah it's a compliment you actually got nice
legs, still
bare toned and that bare smooth
you should let them out more
I almost forgot you know

> *Joy lunges at Kai and they begin to fight.*
> *For just a second it looks a tiny bit*
> *like the looping movement in o.*

(*Getting away.*) RELAX, MAN. CAN NEITHER OF YOU
TAKE A FUCKIN JOKE NO MORE.
JHEEZE.

1

Kai and Khaleem.

Kai I bet you're happy.

Khaleem Move, man.

Kai You've always wanted this to happen.

Khaleem . . .

Kai Waiting and waiting and waiting for the day I get knocked down to your level.

Khaleem What are you talking about?

Kai Who else would tell Mr Tomlin?

Khaleem Oh, you think I snitched.

Kai You did.

Khaleem Don't care enough to report you for selling your stupid masks.

Kai Liar.

Khaleem Relax.

Kai I hate you.

Khaleem Why cos they took away your little badge and someone jacked your stupid scooter and you got put in isolation for the first time in your neeky life.

Kai They interviewed me in Mr Tomlin's office while everyone waited down the corridor listening.

Khaleem I didn't report you for selling your stupid masks.

Kai Well Mr Tomlin called me into his office and emptied them out of my bag and then reported to the police because he thought I'd been recruited into some shit – talking about it's for my own good.

Khaleem Not my problem.

Kai It is your problem. Everyone always thinks we're the same.

Khaleem Well we *are* brothers.

Kai Half-brothers.

Khaleem Okay.

Kai They said to me
We've got you on camera in the area on The Night in Question
same area we found your brother's diary
I said HALF-brother
and then they said
What were you doing so far from home all late and I couldn't tell them so they put my school picture in between their papers and wrote my name and address down.

Khaleem Tell them why you were there then.

Kai I told them the truth I said
I DON'T KNOW
I DON'T KNOW WHY I'M THERE

Khaleem Tell them WHERE you were then.

Kai I don't know.
. . .
Do you fucking know why they've got your diary?

Khaleem Nah.
But I'm not scared cos I know I didn't do nothing.

Kai On the CCTV next to me on The Night in Question they've got Joy. But they haven't got her face properly. And they kept asking me who's that next to you who's that next to you. And I know Joy doesn't know why she's on that camera either and I'm not snitching on her.
. . .
Both of us got futures.

Khaleem Why you afraid if you know you didn't do nothing? If you're scared get your dad to save you, innit.

Kai All of this is your fault.

Khaleem Move, man.

Kai You had to go and take the trainers down you just had to.

You finished yourself time ago and you can't wait for everyone else to be finished like you
doesn't matter if you didn't do nothing they've had your face in between their papers for time they've been waiting to get you they know you've got no future innit so it don't matter anyway you could walk around bait if you wanted cos you've got nothing to protect anyway and you just had to drag the rest of us with you when you finished your self time ago

Khaleem I didn't.

Kai You did.

Khaleem I'M NOT FINISHED.

Kai Yeah you are.

> *Khaleem lunges at Kai and they fight.*
> *It looks somehow like the looping movement from o.*

> *Baitface appears.*
> *He watches them fight.*

> *In their struggle, a beaded bracelet on Khaleem's wrist breaks and the beads spill across the ground.*
> *He stops the fight and gathers them one by one.*

> *Baitface helps Khaleem pick up the beads.*

1

> *Khaleem is alone.*
> *He is carefully, desperately, stringing the beads on his broken bracelet back together.*

> *Joy enters.*
> *Khaleem pulls on his bally.*

Joy Heard Mrs Delaney kicked you out of gospel choir.

Khaleem . . .

Joy Sorry.

Khaleem Fuck off.

Joy . . .
Sorry that you're excluded again.

Khaleem Fuck off.

Joy And sorry about Angel. I know you liked her.

Khaleem FUCK OFF.

o

> *No_Trace polishes the trainer light.*
> *No_Case is fast asleep with the*
> *homework diary close by his head.*

No_Trace You can't.

No_Face I'm going.

No_Trace Where?

No_Face Dunno. Somewhere. Out.
I'll see innit.

No_Trace Don't be silly, G. How you gonna see?

No_Face I'll just see, man.
This don't make sense anyway.

No_Trace You can't just go.

> *No_Case stirs.*

No_Face Don't wake him.

No_Trace You can't just leave and say you're going
going where, G?

No_Face What am I gonna do here just fuckin
this shit

No_Trace What about the dream, man?
The proper light, man?
Just wait.

No_Face You know what's weird about that dream

No_Trace What?

No_Face Now I think about it
that dream about when I saw the light
I thought it was shining on me but it weren't
It was shining behind me like hitting me
bare harsh and I see myself stretched out on the floor
cos all I am is actually just a shadow on the floor
and I turn around and the light is there
bare bright
bare rays
like BARE
like blinding
like penetrating my eyelids
and I can't actually see no more.
like see anything.

No_Trace You can't just leave.
How you gonna sleep?

No_Face Ain't slept in days.

No_Trace What you even trying to find?

No_Face . . .

No_Trace What if the light comes and you miss it?

No_Face Didn't you hear me?
Light ain't shit.

It's been shining.
We're the shadow on the floor, G.

No_Trace How you gonna go?

No_Face I'll walk, innit.

I

The hanging trainers are now mashed up and dirty.
From this point forward, Kai and Khaleem
do not remove their ballys unless stated.
It doesn't matter if we can't differentiate
them from their o doubles.

Khaleem and Joy are waiting.
They've laid down a bouquet of flowers.
Joy is taking off his skirt and putting on a pair of joggers.

Meanwhile, Kai is somewhere else.
He is reading his passport, quietly,
obsessively memorising his name.

Joy Remember that time he sang 'Silent Night' at the
Christmas assembly?

Khaleem Yeah.
Bare tingles in my face after that.
Had to go toilet and slap myself to pattern the goosebumps.

Joy Remember on sports day when he started handing out
his homemade energy drink to everyone in Good House?

Khaleem Still need to know what juj he put in that cos I've
never run so fast in my life.

Joy Abraham; supplier of sauce and sorcery.

Khaleem I'll never understand how can you be there one day and I can see you
and the next day you're just not there no more.

Joy That's how it felt when my mum died. I just kept thinking this don't make sense cos if you're not here then where are you?

Khaleem I'm sorry.

Joy It's okay.

Khaleem Did you cry?

Joy I cry bare.

Khaleem I don't really know how to.

Joy I know.

Khaleem I thought he just had food poisoning, man.
Thought he was gonna be off for one day. Two days max.
Three days if it was from the Stratford KFC.

> *Kai dials Joy's phone number. It rings.*
> *Joy checks it, ignores.*

Khaleem Who's that?

Joy No one.

> *Beat.*
> *Khaleem climbs the wall and taps the hanging trainers.*

Khaleem Hate this shit.
(*To Joy.*) You're lucky you're safe.

Khaleem is waiting for Angel by the school gate.
He sees her and takes off his bally.

Khaleem (*calling for her*) Oi Angel.
Oi Ange!
ANGE, MAN.
ANGEL.
ANGEL.
ANGEL.
IT'S ME.

She ignores him like he is invisible.

He checks his face with his phone camera;
he is not invisible.
He examines the eczema around his nose.
Maybe she does have the ick.
Maybe he's ugly now.

He puts his bally back on.

o

No_Face is alone.

The bassline gets thicker and heavier as he walks
through
and through
and through
and through
the dark.

> *Kai stares up at the hanging trainers.*
> *Joy enters. They're distant, like they haven't spoken in ages.*

Kai (*looking at hanging trainers*) They're dirty.

> *Beat.*

Joy You got what I asked for?

Kai Who's it for?

Joy . . .
My cousin.

Kai What's his name?

Joy . . .
J-Josh.
Clarke. Joshua Clarke.

Kai Whose side?

Joy What?

Kai Whose side of your family is he from?

Joy Why do you need to know?

Kai I like to know who my customers are.

Joy Can I buy one for him or not?

> *Kai hands him a bally. It looks like it's*
> *been made out of a baby blanket.*

. . .
. . .
He wants a different one.

Kai It's all I've got since Mr Tomlin confiscated my stock.

Joy You sure it's fine?

Kai Why wouldn't it be fine?

Joy Cos of Kaleb.

Kai It's fine. He's a baby, he's got bare blankets. His blankets have blankets.

Joy How much?

Kai Free.

Joy Nah. How much.

Kai Free, we're cool.

> *Joy throws a five-pound note down and leaves.*
> *They are not cool.*

J!
PLEASE!
I said I'm sorry . . .

o

> *The trainer light is off because no one is polishing.*
> *The bassline is thick, scary, mad again.*

> *No_Case and No_Trace are in the*
> *looping movement with each other.*
> *No_Trace is trying really hard*
> *to restrain his terror of the dark,*
> *concentrating on the words.*

No_Case Zodiac

No_Trace Zillion

No_Case Zillionaire

No_Trace Zoo

No_Case Zoology

No_Trace Zoologist

No_Case Zeitgeist

No_Trace Zucchini

No_Case Zombie

No_Trace Zombify

No_Case Zombification

No_Trace Zap

No_Case Zappy

No_Trace Zappier

No_Trace Zappiest

No_Case See I told you. It works.
Just try not to feel nothing and you're fine.
Dark's only scary if you let yourself feel it.

No_Trace Zig

No_Case Zag

No_Trace Zed

I

Joy is walking home.
The security alarm ringing in his ears is incessant.
He rubs his ears to make it stop.
It only gets louder and louder.

Baitface appears, takes Joy's baby blanket bally off
and replaces it with one that renders his face
completely invisible.

Joy runs home.

Khaleem waits outside Angel's house, barefaced.
He throws stones up at her window.

Khaleem (*calling for her*) Oi Angel.
Oi Ange!
Please.
I love you.
ANGE, MAN.
ANGEL.
ANGEL.
ANGEL.
IT'S ME.

A siren light nearby flashes blue.
He stops. Puts on his bally.

AY YOU'RE MOVING MAD NOW.
YOU THINK YOU'RE BAD, INNIT.
YOU'RE A SKET ANYWAY.
BITCH.

○

The bassline is thick, scary, mad.
No_Face is still alone.

He is still walking
through
and through
and through
and through
the dark.

The trainer light is still off.
The bassline is thick, scary, mad.

No_Case and No_Trace are stuck in the
looping movement with each other.
It is has become much larger and darker.
They do not need to see each other.
They cannot stop if they try.

I

Kai, Khaleem and Joy.

Kai notices Joy wearing a bally, but doesn't ask.

Kai Angel told me she's gonna go to the police.

Khaleem And say what?

Kai She's gonna give a statement.

Khaleem About what?

Kai She's gonna say she saw you on The Night in Question near The Scene of The Crime on the news on the top deck of the N86 and you told her you'd done something bad.

Khaleem . . .

Kai And that you've been harassing her cos you know she knows.

Khaleem . . .
Let her go then.

Joy Did she?

Khaleem What?

Joy Did she see you?

Khaleem How many times do I have to say it?
I DON'T REMEMBER.

Kai Try.

Khaleem YOU TRY.
HOW ARE YOU THERE IF YOU DON'T REMEMBER?

Kai I don't know.

Khaleem (*to Joy*) WHAT ABOUT YOU?

Joy I don't know I don't know

Khaleem DON'T YOU THINK IF I KNEW I WOULD SAY
SOMETHING SO THEY WOULD CROSS MY FACE OFF
THEIR STUPID LIST?

Kai She said she's gonna go tonight.
If she goes you're finished.
And then I'm finished because of you.

Khaleem JUST SAY YOU THINK I DID SOMETHING.

Kai (*to Joy; panicking*) Just try remember just try remember
FUCKING TRY you're the only one that can help just try
it can't touch you take that fuckin thing off your face you
don't even need it man it can't touch you you know just
tell us

Joy HOW MANY TIMES DO I HAVE TO TELL YOU
MAN BEFORE YOU LISTEN TO ME
I DON'T –

o

The trainer light is still off.
The bassline is still thick, scary, mad.

No_Case and No_Trace are still stuck
in the looping movement with each other.
It is huge now.

No_Face is still alone.
He is still walking
through
and through
and through
and through
the dark.

Then, out of nowhere,
he sees a LIGHT coming towards him in the distance.

I

The bassline is thick, scary, mad.

Baitface appears.
He watches them:
Kai and Joy are stuck in the looping movement
with each other; large and dark.
Khaleem is alone.

They rotate.

*Joy and Khaleem are stuck in the looping movement
with each other; large and dark.
Kai is alone.*

They rotate.

*Khaleem and Kai are stuck in the looping movement
with each other; large and dark.
Joy is alone.*

They rotate.

*Kai and Joy are stuck in the looping movement
with each other; large and dark.
Khaleem is alone.*

(It feels like this pattern goes on forever)

*Baitface takes off one of his socks and uses it to
cover the lens of one of the CCTV cameras:*

*Joy is released from the camera's ray,
and from the movement.
He snaps out of it.
He emits light.*

Joy He's over there.

*Baitface takes off his other sock and uses it to
cover the lens of the second CCTV camera:*

*Kai is released from the camera's ray,
and from the movement.*

> *He snaps out of it.*
> *He emits light.*

Kai Raaaah that's mad.

> *They flash back to:*

THE NIGHT IN QUESTION (CONTINUED)

> *Kai and Joy emit light.*
> *We see Khaleem through CCTV camera light.*

> *Khaleem is alone, bally on, sitting on a wall.*
> *He is writing something in his homework diary.*

> *Kai and Joy appear close by.*
> *They both have ballys on.*

Joy He's over there.

Kai (*noticing Joy's covered face; amused*) Raaaah that's mad.

Joy ...

Kai I must be tripping bare cos you're wearing one as well.

> *Khaleem notices them.*

Khaleem Why you man here?

> *Khaleem notices Joy's covered face.*
> *For a beat they see each other.*
> *He says nothing about it.*

> *Kai looks closely at Khaleem's wrist,*
> *and sees the beaded bracelet.*
> *He grabs Khaleem's wrist to feel it.*

Kai I knew it was real.

Khaleem Get off me, man.

Joy Leave him. He's fried.

Khaleem Did you follow me here?

Kai Nah we're waiting for
(*Mouthing the unspeakable.*) 'BAITFACE'.

> *Khaleem looks up at the hanging trainers;*
> *like 'You're joking right?'*

Daredevil tings went a bit left innit.
Went under by accident. Massive L.
Joy heard about a way to reverse it. Skrrrt.
The ting brought us here innit.
We just have to wait for the Gullyman to show his face.

Khaleem How high are you lot?

Joy It's to connect us to the fifth dimension, bro.

Khaleem How you gonna know?

Joy The feeling innit.

Kai The spirit.

> *Beat.*
> *They wait.*

Joy (*to Khaleem*) Were you crying?

Khaleem Nah.

> *Kai snatches Khaleem's homework diary out of his hands.*
> *Climbs the wall so Khaleem can't reach him.*

OI, MAN.

> *Kai flips through the diary, reading.*

Kai Ai gimme a beat gimme a beat gimme a beat gimme a beat

> *Joy gives him a beat.*

I said
wagwarn bebé
can't ya
tell dat I'm crazé
ya said I'm
makin ya hate mé
but I been
missin ya latelé

Khaleem Do you want me to box your head?

Kai Honest opinion I think we need a bit more wordplay.
You need to make the peopledem wanna rewind the ting
you get me?

Joy Yeah yeah yeah metaphors and similes innit.

Kai Imagery and hyperbole innit.
Like Dave.

Khaleem (*not in the mood*) Give me the ting, man.

Kai Aight aight aight relax relax
relaxation inna sunshine vacation

Khaleem takes the diary back.

Joy It's about Angel innit. Angel from gospel choir?

Khaleem . . .

Kai Look at him. Aww. Sprung like a spring chicken.

Khaleem Can you lot just leave me alone.

Joy Saw her just now coming off the N86 just after you.
. . .
Why were you crying?

Khaleem I told you I wasn't.

Kai Oh shit, he got curved.

Khaleem I didn't get curved I wasn't crying.

Joy Nah but you wanted to. You should've just cried.

Khaleem Leave it yeah.

>> *Beat.*
>> *They wait.*

Kai What if this doesn't work?

Joy We've done it. Just wait.

Kai What time is it?

Joy Eleven past one.

Kai Surely we should've heard his voice by now??

Kai Maybe it doesn't matter.
If we don't reverse it my dad's gonna finish me before
Baitface does.

Joy Just wait.

Kai How do you know it works?

>> *Beat.*
>> *They wait.*
>> *Nothing.*
>> *Kai's panic increases.*

It's not gonna work we didn't do it right it's not gonna
fucking work I'm finished

Joy We did it right.

Kai How do you know you don't know nothing about this
how are you gonna know anything about this

Joy I KNOW, MAN.
I KNOW WE DID IT RIGHT COS I HAVE TO KNOW IT
TOO.

>> *Beat.*

How many times do I have to tell you.
How is it harder for you man to accept who I am than it is
for my dad?

At least he believes me. He doesn't make me explain it over and over.

You think I don't know what it's like? I know what it's like and I know what it means. I just don't wanna have to wear this fucking thing on my face all the time.

Kai G, none of us want to wear it but it's not really a choice out here.

Joy I KNOW THAT.

Kai Just tell her Khaleem she don't understand.

Khaleem Bro.

Joy . . .

Kai I'm sorry. I didn't mean it like that. I'm not used to it yet. I'm sorry.

Beat.
They wait.

Khaleem You're right I wanted to cry but I didn't.
My gran died.
Just now.
Been going to her flat on Fridays, we're watching *Come Dine With Me* from season one.
Was. We was.
I thought she just fell asleep in the adverts but when I tried to wake her up she didn't.
I didn't know what to do.
It was just me there. I didn't know.
So I just left I didn't even call the ambulance or nothing.
I should've. I just left. Like I thought if I just leave then it didn't happen
and she'll be there when I go next Friday.

Then I got on the N86 and sat on the top deck on my ones and two stops in Angel gets on
and sits next to me for no reason when there's bare other seats and that's when I should've just cried.

93

I didn't even tell her nothing about my gran cos all I could think was no one's ever sat next to me on a night bus before.

Kai . . .

Joy . . .

Kai Rah.
(*Suggesting the beaded bracelet.*) Your gran gave you that didn't she?

Khaleem Yeah.

Kai . . .
. . .
. . .
Can't believe you got chicken and chips after that.

Joy Kai.

Kai Sorry.

Joy Khaleem, we should call the ambulance.

Khaleem You do it please.

> *Khaleem hands Joy his phone.*
> *He goes to climb the wall.*

Kai (*to Khaleem*) What you doing?

Khaleem I forgot I haven't touched it today.

> *Khaleem climbs the wall and taps the hanging trainers.*

> *A woman on the street sees them.*
> *Three black figures in balaclavas.*
> *She slows down, then crosses the road, terrified of them.*

> *Joy dials 999.*   *The woman dials 999.*
>   *Both lines ring.*

Operator Emergency, what service do you require?

The boys see the woman with her phone to her ear.

They freeze. They try not to make any sudden movements.
They watch her as nervously as she watches them.

Do you require the fire service?
Or do you require ambulance or police?

It's a tense stare-down, thick with fear on both sides.

Ambulance or *Police*?

Joy hangs up his line.
The woman doesn't hang up hers.

If you are in an emergency and unable to speak please tap
the handset or make a noise.

Operator waits. Silence.

If you're unable to speak, press five-five and your call will
be transferred to the police.

The woman dials 55.

Kai's stomach grumbles.
The woman faints.

Kai (*whispering*) Shit.
The weed made me hungry, man.

Police Operator Metropolitan Police, what's your
emergency?

Khaleem is frozen, standing on the wall
underneath the trainers.

Joy rushes towards the woman to help.
Kai pulls him back.
They scuffle:

Joy What you doing?

Kai You can't just go over there man.

Joy We have to help.

Kai Stop.
THINK FOR ONE SECOND, MAN.

> (*This is the origination of the looping
> movement that we see in CCTV/o.*)
> *Then Khaleem feels the CCTV camera pointing directly
> under the trainers; at him.*

> *Baitface, who has been lingering, removes his bally
> and uses it to cover the third CCTV camera.
> Khaleem is released from the camera's ray.
> He snaps out of the flashback,
> into the present:*

I

> *Khaleem sees Baitface for the first time.
> He stares at the spirit, otherworldly.*

o

> *Baitface glows with white light. No_Face sees him.
> (He's the light that was coming in the distance.)*

> *No_Face is a little scared.
> Baitface checks him.*

Baitface Who are you?

No_Face No one bro, I'm just walking.

Baitface Where you from?

No_Face Round here.

Baitface How come I've never seen you before?

No_Face I dunno, bro I'm just walking.
. . .
Who are you?

Baitface Just walking.

No_Face Why ain't you got shoes?

Baitface Why ain't you got a face?
. . .
Dickhead.

No_Face Dunno.

Baitface Are you alone?

No_Face Yeah.

Baitface Why?

No_Face . . .
Zed.

Baitface Why?

No_Face Zed.

Baitface Why?

No_Face Cos I left.

Baitface You like being alone?

No_Face Nah

Baitface But you left?

No_Face Yeah

Baitface Why?

No_Face Zed.

Baitface Why?

No_Face Zed.

Baitface Why did you leave?

No_Face Cos I'm scared, innit.
I'm scared this is all there is and nothing's ever gonna
happen and there's no seen feeling.
And if this is all there is and nothing's ever gonna happen
and there's no seen feeling
then there's no point dreaming any more.

Baitface Rah . . . that's deep, still.
But I can't lie, I been walking for time
and I don't think nothing's ever gonna happen round here
either, bro.
At least where you came from you weren't alone.

No_Face . . .
Why *you* been walking?

Baitface Just tryna find my fucking shoes.

I

Where we left off:
Khaleem is seeing Baitface for the first time.
Kai and Joy haven't noticed the spirit yet.

Kai I think remember what happened that night.

Joy Me too.
We ran away.

Kai And then we went back to Khaleem's gran's house and
called the ambulance.

Joy That's why they found his diary.

Kai How did we forget all of that?

Khaleem Ay, you man . . .
You man, look.

> *Kai and Joy see Baitface for the first time.*
> *They are stunned.*

Kai Is that . . . ?

Joy I think so . . .

Khaleem Baitface.

> *Beat.*

Kai We come in peace . . .

Joy He's not a fuckin alien.

Kai What is he then??

Joy I dunno.

Khaleem (*carefully*) I'm sorry . . .
For taking the trainers down.
I didn't mean to make you angry and I put them back straight after.

Joy We take full responsibility.

Kai (*to Joy*) *We* didn't do nothing.

Khaleem (*kneeling*) Please don't curse me.

Joy (*to Baitface*) Please, man. Allow it. He's grieving. He's still at stage one.

Kai Yeah. And we're his support system, so don't curse us either.

Baitface . . .

Kai Can he talk?

> *Baitface climbs up to get the hanging trainers down.*
> *The boys squirm.*

Khaleem PLEASE! **Joy** NAH!

Kai WE'RE TOO YOUNG TO DIE!

Baitface hands Khaleem the trainers.
Khaleem takes them, reluctantly.
Baitface gestures for him to read the inside label.
He does:

Khaleem (*reading*) Babatunde Michaels.
George Grierson Academy.
Nine-B.
Good House.
2004.

Baitface . . .

Khaleem Was that you?

Baitface nods.

Kai You were in Good House?

Baitface nods.

Joy We're in Good House.

Kai If you let us live, I promise I will personally make sure Good House wins sports day for the next three years.

Khaleem How did you die?

Baitface . . .

Baitface points at the CCTV cameras.
Then he takes the trainers back from Khaleem
and throws them back up on the wire.
He points at the trainers, then back at the covered cameras;
he's trying to tell them something.

Kai I don't get it.

Joy Listen.

Khaleem finally understands.
He takes off his bally and walks
underneath the trainers, he looks up.

Kai What are you doing?!

Khaleem He's been protecting us.

. . .

He's not cursing us.

Kai What?

Khaleem Don't walk under the shoes Baitface or you'll get Baitfaced.
But it's not the shoes, is it . . . ?
He's not the one cursing us. He's just showing us where not to . . .
He's always been good.

> *Joy realises and takes off his bally.*
> *Baitface signs a sentence in a*
> *made-up black boy sign language.*

Kai What is he saying?

Joy (*reading*) Don't give them your face or they'll take it . . .

. . .

Big light . . .
You look like big light . . .
. . . God? Light?
Too much God?
Too much light?
So much light.

> *Baitface nods.*
> *Kai understands and takes off his bally.*
>
> *Baitface signs another sentence.*

Khaleem . . .

Khaleem Yeah?

Joy He says your gran says hi.

> *Khaleem cries for the first time in the whole play.*

I know how you feel, bro.

> *Baitface signs another sentence.*

Kai . . .

Kai Yeah?

Joy He says you got something to say to me.

Kai Have I?

> *Baitface nods.*
> *Kai hesitates, then apologetically walks up to Joy.*

I'm sorry for what I said about your legs.

> *Baitface signs.*

Joy He says AND . . .

Kai Are you taking the piss?

Joy Bro that's what he said.

Kai AND . . .
I wanted to say . . .
Thank you for protecting me that night.
And . . . I love you innit . . .
But not like that . . .
I love you cos you're . . . you're you so . . .
I wanted to ask . . . can we be boys again?

Joy . . .
Yeah, boys.

> *They spud.*
> *Baitface signs: HUG.*

He says we should hug.

Kai Are you serious?

Joy Yeah. He said it in caps lock.

> *They hug.*

> *Baitface goes to take his socks*
> *and bally off the CCTV cameras.*

Khaleem Okay, we gotta put them back on now.

> *Kai and Joy are still hugging.*

Kai We're not done.

Khaleem Back to reality.
Pattern yourselves.

> *They finish the hug and put their ballys back on.*
> *Baitface takes his socks and bally*
> *off the cameras and puts them on.*

> *The CCTV rays begin to shine again.*

o

> *For some reason, it's quiet.*

> *No_Case and No_Trace are in the dark,*
> *still stuck in the looping movement with each other.*
> *The movement is still large and dark.*

> *No_Face enters with Baitface, who is glowing.*

> *No_Case and No_Trace stop and look.*

No_Case . . .

No_Trace . . .

No_Case You came back?

No_Face I didn't mean to.

No_Trace . . .

No_Face I just kept walking away further and further and
further got me back to you, bro.

No_Case Like a circle?

No_Face ...

No_Trace Madting.

No_Case Who's that?

Baitface No one, G. I was just walking.

No_Trace You too?

No_Face Said he's looking for his shoes.

> *No_Face points at the hanging trainers.*

Do they look like that?

Baitface ...
Yeah, think so.

> *No_Face climbs up and gets the trainers down for Baitface.*
> *Baitface puts the trainers on.*

> *Then immediately there's*

BIG LIGHT
PROPER LIGHT
SO MUCH LIGHT
TOO MUCH LIGHT
EVERYWHERE!!!

No_Case Rah.

No_Trace Rah.

No_Face Mad.

No_Case Mad.

No_Trace Mad.

No_Case (*to No_Face*) Is this how we're shining in your dream?

No_Face Yeah, G.

END.

(*A maybe scene, this can also play as the audience exit.*)

The CCTV footage from pp. 23–24 is replayed but now the evidence is completely corrupted by LIGHT:

The CCTV footage obtained by the Metropolitan Police that was understood to show [

] suspected of A Crime committed against a Vulnerable Victim in One Borough of London on A Date Not Too Long Ago, has been deemed inadmissible after becoming mysteriously corrupted by what appears to be very bright light.

I'm joined now by our Crime correspondent Terry Davis for more. Terry what can you tell us about this [

]

Again, police are examining the CCTV footage of the three [

] who appeared close to The Scene of The Crime on The Night in Question.

The footage has undergone rigorous forensic analysis but, as you can see, no one can explain how or why it became corrupted.

This does however mean that, as you said, the prime piece of evidence connecting the three [

] to The Crime is, in fact, inadmissible.